A SOCIOPATH BESIDE ME

by
Junie Moon

Edited by Joseph R. Miller, M.D.

ISBN 978-1937520-56-4
Published by First Edition Design Publishing
February 2012
www.firsteditiondesignpublishing.com

Library of Congress Control Number
2012932463

Disclaimer

The author and publisher of this book and the accompanying materials have used their best efforts in preparing this book. The author and publisher make no representation or warranties with respect to the accuracy, applicability, fitness, or completeness of the contents of this book. The information contained in this book is strictly for educational and enjoyment purposes. Therefore, if you wish to apply ideas contained in this book, you are taking full responsibility for your actions.

The author and publisher disclaim any warranties (express or implied), merchantability, or fitness for any particular purpose. The author and publisher shall in no event be held liable to any party for any direct, indirect, punitive, special, incidental or other consequential damages arising directly or indirectly from any use of this material, which is provided "as is", and without warranties.

I began to edit A Sociopath Beside Me as a favor for a friend. I ended the task with a feeling of sadness that the job was done, and that I wouldn't be able to learn more about Marvin or Joseph or any of the lost souls I had learned of in the book. What began simply as a favor crawled inside me and took me over for a while. While it was there inside me, it caused me pain. I began to fear the sociopath I was writing of, and I realized the author had done what good authors do: she had described a personal feeling and translated that feeling from personal to communal. In short, she made me feel it too. She will do that for any reader who picks this up and reads it through. You will experience fear, and wonder, and anger, and you will be afraid. That's what the author intends. Be afraid. Be very afraid.

Joseph R. Miller, M.D.

I first met Junie several years after her experiences with a sociopath. After we became friends, she told me her story. She was visibly upset while telling me the story. I suggested it might help her heal if she wrote it all down. She was reluctant, so I told her, just do it. Several years later, she presented me with a hand written book that she had written. She told me it was her desire to publish this book so others may read it and become aware of the danger signs of a sociopath. The book read like a movie or TV show, but I knew Junie and knew the story to be true. I believe she has accomplished her mission and the book "A Sociopath Beside Me" is now a published eBook. After I read the book, I was able to look back in my past and realize that sociopaths that had crossed my path had victimized me many times. I am now well armed with the tools to avoid any future encounters with a Sociopath. Good job Junie, thanks for a job well done.

Gary Bennett

From the Author

Because of this journey
I have learned so much,
and despite of it
I have come so far...

Special Thanks:

A special thank you to the following people who without their creative abilities, determination and confidence in this project this book would not exist.

To Gary-

My advisor, mentor and friend, who unknowingly encouraged the creation of this book by inspiring me with just two small but very profound words, "do it!" Those words were a turning point for me. Along the way he became a believer in this force for good and became my computer expert, publisher, marketing agent and all around rock. Without you, this work would still be in handwritten form, collecting dust somewhere. Thank you, Gary.

To Joe-

Who volunteered his editing and authoring skills that took this diamond in the rough and polished it into a treasure. Without even being aware, his wise words of "without details it isn't a story," helped push me out of the writers nest and transformed me into an author. Thank you Joe, I am forever grateful.

Junie Moon

To Marvin
To His Family
To Joseph

Note from the author...

You have met a predator. He has crossed your path and you didn't even know. Why did he pass you by? Why did he look at someone else? Most likely he sought someone who could better satisfy his cravings. You were lucky.

This predator, this hunter on the prowl, is the human equivalent of a Great White Shark. He is a sociopath, as strictly defined in psychiatric literature. He is a menace without conscience, and like the shark in the ocean, he will eat you alive before you sense the danger. You need only cross his path. I had the great misfortune to know intimately a sociopath for eighteen years. It took too many of those years to recognize the problem. For the rest of those years, my professional training in observation and analysis were put to the ultimate test.

My hope for this book is to give you the tools to recognize the sociopath and his behavior. Only by this recognition can you see the sociopath for what he really is, and by seeing what he really is, protect yourself and others from the pain of his intrusion.

Expect the unexpected, think the unthinkable...but recognize what is happening. It took a terrible, eighteen year journey with a sociopath by my side to first understand then withstand the sociopath's power. My desire is to share this understanding with you, to have you use this book as a guide to recognizing these dark souls. I hope it contains the tools and armor that will protect you and help you avoid being victimized by a sociopath beside you.

This is a true story; it contains real events, events that caused great emotional pain to real people.

Names have been changed and the predator's relationships with his victims, including this author, are intentionally vague to protect the confidentiality of those involved.

On the victim's behalf, some of the proceeds from the sale of this book will be donated toward efforts in locating and bringing to justice their perpetrator.

The Author

ACKNOWLEDGEMENTS

To the many victims of the sociopath who walked beside me:

I wish for each one of you to know that what he chose to do to you was not your fault. A sociopath is only interested in meeting his own agenda through nearly any means possible, and we, as society, are merely his pawns. He chose you simply because he knew you. For each of you I wish the courage and the wisdom to release any emotional hold he may still have upon you. I wish you comfort and peace.

To the truth:

Which is still buried beneath his many dark untruths, I want to bring light. Your well-deserved and rightful voice can bring sunlight, the best disinfectant, and can validate the truth. It can be a healing catalyst for a sociopath's many victims.

And to you the reader:

I want you to be made aware that individuals, as described within these pages, do exist in large numbers. I do not want to alarm you, but to alert you. My hope is that some good can be discovered and salvaged from the trail of destruction the sociopath beside me created and left his victims to contend with. I pray my personal journey can provide you with information and tools that you both deserve and need in becoming more aware of your surroundings and the people who surround you. I hope this will be a decent persons' guide to the indecency of the sociopath beside you.

FOREWORD

I am neither a writer nor a psychiatrist, but have had the personal misfortune of intimately knowing one of society's hidden predators - a sociopath - and am relating the events of living that terrible misfortune to you in my own laymen terms.

I spent the good part---the bad part, if you will---of eighteen years with a sociopath beside me. On many occasions, I found myself wondering, "Whatever was he thinking?" I experienced numerous "red flag" moments. I didn't see them as other than just plain odd. I didn't put the pieces together at the time strange things happened. I shrugged the vague unrest away, unwilling to think the unthinkable, unable to visualize the unexpected. I couldn't put the pieces of the puzzle together until long after the incidents occurred.

When I could not make sense of these instances in my own mind, I would probe for an explanation. In retrospect, my probing was too gentle. Each explanation led me to more confusion. I received no satisfactory answers. I ended each episode with more unanswered questions, and a deeper sense that something wasn't right.

My rational mind prodded me to investigate and not to turn a blind eye to his inconsistencies. My emotional self would not allow me to do that. I had physical symptoms including stomach pain, warnings such as the bristling of the hairs on the nape of my neck. My intuition prodded me not to turn a blind eye, but for the longest time, I did just that. It was as if I suspected a monster lived in the closet, but if I never opened the closet door, no one else would know. I cannot point to a specific moment in time when suspicion piled up past believing. But such a time did arrive, and I couldn't rationalize his strange behavior, could no longer give him the benefit of the doubt. I reached that point where my rational and emotional selves merged in protest to his lies. I would no longer allow him to make me feel guilty for questioning him. I could no longer live on trust. From that point forward, I walked a fragile line, aware that if I probed too openly he would become suspicious and stop communicating entirely. I did not want to kill the messenger until the message became clear.

During this time we lived together in several different towns. An uncomfortable knowledge was building in my mind. My heart told me that to ignore these continuing red flag moments would have devastating effects down the line. But it was always "somewhere down the line." We continued our own fragile personal dance. There were little dots of information from things he said or comments from those around him. I tried to connect the dots but wouldn't let my mind see purpose in the results.

Then came the phone call – the one that none of us could ever be prepared for, the one that, in an instant, propels you into a living nightmare. The phone call opened the closet door of the sociopath beside me, and his hidden dirty little secrets tumbled into the daylight. Secrets that weren't even supposed to see the light of day. It took all my courage to hear these secrets. It frightened me that I had missed the signs. How could I have missed them? How could I have been so blind? And most frightening of all was the idea that I had allowed his reign of psychological terror by refusing to see the signs.

I began my quest to know the painful truth of each occurrence and how each incident began. I continue this so you might recognize the sociopath beside you.

Contents

Chapter One - The Sociopath 1
Chapter Two - Dark Soul 3
Chapter Three - Master Of Disguise 9
Chapter Four - Hunter On The Hunt 13
Chapter Five - Lies, Lies, And More Lies 17
Chapter Six - The Closet 19
Chapter Seven - The Phone Call 21
Chapter Eight - Silencing The Truth 27
Chapter Nine - Fallen 31
Chapter Ten - Ben 35
Chapter Eleven - Constant Companions 41
Chapter Twelve - The Non-Intimate Relationship 43
Chapter Thirteen - Penny 45
Chapter Fourteen - Penny's Struggle 53
Chapter Fifteen - Malignant 57
Chapter Sixteen - Eddie 59
Chapter Seventeen - Joseph 65
Chapter Eighteen - Justice For None 73

Chapter One
THE SOCIOPATH

It has been estimated that one in twenty-five Americans has shown sociopathic behavior. Despite its frequency, most of us know nothing of that behavior, nor are we aware of sociopaths in our society. This is the sociopath's greatest advantage. He is invisible.

These individuals are afflicted with what is defined as an "antisocial personality disorder". "Antisocial" means simply "against society". The true sociopath's only agenda and main source of his twisted gratification is manipulating those in his path to do as he requires. That's his game. And game it is, with us as pawns as he seeks personal gratification, regardless of the cost to others. His capabilities are monstrous.

He does not follow societies "norms", and is incapable of playing by the rules. He has no rules, nor can he recognize other's rules. He does not have a conscience. Thus, he has no brake on socially unacceptable behavior, no boundary past which he dare not go. The sociopath lacks a moral compass. He cannot experience guilt. He knows no remorse. His life is simply endless sinister manipulation of others to feed his own ego.

When confronted with a sociopath's random acts of cruelty, all you can expect is the unexpected. And of course that can't be done. Only in retrospect is the unexpected visible. You are forced to think the unthinkable. That can't be done as well, except in the light of retrospection. A sociopath has no emotional attachment to others. He has no empathy, no compassion. He lives in emotional disconnect with others, his mind acknowledging nothing but personal goals. He cannot accept responsibility for dishonorable actions, but finds great personal satisfaction in causing others to suffer emotional pain. Simply put, the sociopath cannot accept or even understand the concept of personal responsibility.

He lives a loveless existence, unable and unwilling to bond with another being. He is incapable of gratitude or loyalty toward anyone. His quest in life is to meet his agenda of the moment, without regard for others, indeed, with contempt for his victims.

Individuals with severe personality disorders rarely improve. With no capacity for self-awareness, they most often aren't salvageable. Rehabilitation is a myth.

The sociopath becomes more antisocial with the passing of time. Through years of practice, his manipulation techniques become increasingly more refined and sophisticated. Eventually he regards himself as smarter than everyone else. He becomes increasingly brazen and callused. He knows he will never be caught. This is his game. You are his game-piece. There are no boundaries, no rules to a macabre game that increases in intensity and becomes more disturbing every time you're forced to play.

Chapter Two
DARK SOUL

Your intuition
is your window
into another's soul...

When I first met Marvin I was drawn into his web by his level of intelligence and charismatic charm. His aptitude to articulate was well executed and skillful, nearly flawless, and superior to most 26 year olds. Regardless of the circumstances or the timing, he appeared to never be caught off-guard or at a loss for just the right set of discriminating words to bestow upon the listener; illustrating his gifted "silver tongue" and razor sharp mind.

Without fail, he seemed to be able to charm others to obtain his desired outcome; the ability to mold both people and situations as if they were putty in his hands. It was unusual for someone of his then young age to not only possess these special qualities, but to have mastered them in such a way, that in combination, they orchestrated compliance from his intended target and struck a sense of awe in any observer.

Marvin portrayed the uncanny ability to weave the qualities of impeccable articulation and disarming charm into a carefully woven trap, much like the network of webs spun by a spider, designed for the entanglement of his prey. He was a smiling, gracious, danger.

At the time, it seemed harmless enough as I was totally unaware of his hidden personality traits or sinister, self-serving, agenda. He was a sales representative, and seemed to have the uncanny ability to sell ice to Eskimos. Unfortunately he became part of my inner circle for the next eighteen years, a then budding sociopath. For most of those eighteen years, I didn't recognize the sociopath beside me. The daily routine seemed for the most part, right. I saw nothing out of the ordinary early in our life together. I suspected nothing.

Then the truth was revealed to me, and his elaborate charade exposed. For three years I spent nearly every waking moment and many sleepless nights dissecting and microscopically analyzing every questionable detail of the past.

With the knowledge that I now had, I painfully tried to recall and vividly reconstructed every "red flag" moment that had occurred during the past eighteen years. Hundreds of random thoughts and questions ran through my mind like gingerbread men, crying "catch me. Catch me if you can." Some I caught and some I didn't, and some just flew away.

All these fragments flew through my consciousness.

I did not know this person at all!

Who was this person, really?

Why didn't I see and recognize the signs?

How could he commit such heinous acts toward others with total disregard and even contempt, and why didn't I know sooner?

Why had I been so ignorant of his actions?

How come I did not know?

How could he have duped me? How did he pull the wool over my eyes?

Why didn't I know? Why didn't I know?

How could I protect myself and those I love from him and "his kind" now and in the future?

Again and always the question raced through my mind. Why didn't I know? I prayed daily for the wisdom and courage to find the truth, but still was filled with dread.

To begin to find the truth, I used what I had learned from him, from being in his presence, from living with him beside me. I began to get information from others. I began the laborious process of connecting the dots. The road to truth was painful. The truth was more often than not buried in his closet of dirty secrets. I dreaded the pain of entering that closet. I feared what I would find. Each discovery was foreign to my nature, nearly impossible to comprehend. My mind and my senses were assaulted by another world, the world of a sociopath. I was nauseated by what I found. I sobbed with sorrow for the pain he caused his victims. But in spite of the personal pain, I persisted. His secrets, his plan of operation unfolded. I was unable to comprehend his motives. I could not rationalize them. They were devoid of reason and outside of ordered, rational thought. They were outside my experience.

I was faced with a daunting task. How could I understand his reasoning and rationale when no boundaries existed, when there were no guidelines in my reasoning and reasonable mind trained to examine the unreasonable? I had to crawl inside his mind, inside his heart, and enter his soul. In effect, I had to become him in order to understand this emerging monster that had lived beside me. How could I do that and maintain my own sanity? How dangerous was the road to discovery? Would I be destroyed by trying to think as he did?

To maintain my sanity, to reinforce to myself that I was rational and clear thinking and not drifting down his monstrous path, I pretended it was all a bad dream. I tried to do that, but there were times I could not. Even on the best of days, I was aware that the insanity was real, and coming from a real mind, albeit the mind of a sick and irrational sociopath. Think about that for a moment. How do you enter insanity with a sane mind and not fall over the edge? I kept thinking of his many victims and the terrible things they must have endured. It was the hardest thing I have ever done. So many times I had to stop and weep. But I began with little steps, starting with a re-examination of the past behaviors that I could remember. The small steps got larger. More and more of his past behavior did not survive strict study of the facts. I had let my rational self-protective self, override my emotions too long. I had to learn to let my emotional self loose, to follow where it led me, then see if what I thought was simply an emotional quirk was really something more. I began my journey into the sociopathic mind. I looked evil in the face and tried to stare it down.

I began to question all his past behaviors. There were many red-flag moments that stood out. There were many moments that were not flagged, but seemed within the realm of normal at the time they happened. But in retrospect, they didn't seem to fit the actions of their time. I had to revert to my training as a psychiatric nurse and use great force of will so I could start to put the pieces of this terrible puzzle in perspective. I searched for hidden pieces of the puzzle, clues that I had overlooked, or looked away from in order to protect myself.

When they occurred, the fraud and deceptions were so perfectly orchestrated that they effectively disguised the truth. I realized I had been deceived. I was always an unwilling victim. But there were times I must have knowingly turned away. I described earlier the hairs standing on the nape of my neck. At those times, did I turn from the truth in order to protect myself? What he did was so perfectly orchestrated that the truth was effectively disguised. Still, there had to have been times I closed my eyes because the truth was so despicable. I refused to look evil in the eye at times, because the pain was far too great. How could I not have known? That question recurs. It haunts me still. I live with that pain today. But I know that I was sane then. I know I am sane now. I was an unknowing victim then. I refuse to be one now, and I continue to work on my personal healing process.

I questioned myself then as I do today. Who was this person who appeared to comfort me and care for me? Was I just an oblivious pawn in his plan to deceive, or was it my fault? Was it even partly my fault? Over and over, again and still, I look for things I could have seen or done differently. But that's part of the sociopath's plan. He defers guilt to those around him. He manipulates and twists so others feel the pain while he smiles and continues his macabre game.

I had to learn to think like him. In order to find the truth, I had to go inside his mind. If I did not muster up the courage for that frightful step, I could never learn how all this happened. I could never understand its meaning. I had to take that step. I had to understand his thinking. I had to see inside his soul. If I were ever to help myself and others, I had to see inside the twisted labyrinth within his head; I had to understand why he did the things he did. What I discovered on this agonizing journey took my breath away. At times my blood ran cold. I stared directly in the face of cold, calculating, evil. Perhaps most frightening of all, I found no motivation for the evil acts that he committed. He committed his unnatural crimes against nature simply because he could. It seemed his actions came from another world. Nothing on the surface of his life was at it seemed. He was terribly adept at covering up his real intentions. His family and his friends never realized that he was a fraud. There was an ulterior motive and hidden agenda to everything he did. All his actions were camouflaged so he could continue undetected, unnoticed, and uninterrupted; so he could continue his steady stream of preying on others for his own twisted amusement.

My mission is to paint you the clearest possible picture of the mind of a sociopath, to help you recognize the darkness of his soul. I will share what I have learned, what I have experienced on this dreadful journey. Perhaps I can keep you from the pain of unsuspecting victimization. It is a terrible pain. First it comes from elsewhere, from the sociopath who plays with your mind. Finally, he accomplishes his will, and you heap pain upon yourself. It's not a conscious act, but the pain is real. It's part of his plan. It's what the sociopath beside you intended. It's what Marvin wanted, all along.

Chapter Three
MASTER OF DISGUISE

Is there a central defense against these masters of disguise? How can we avoid becoming trapped in his personal agenda? How can we avoid the sociopath beside us, or living near us, or only passing through? How can we disarm him? The answer is both simple and complex nearly past understanding. See him for what he is. That is our central defense. That is our main weapon to keep us out of his clutches, to avoid or disarm the sociopath's agenda. It is essential you recognize the signs and symptoms of this personality disorder.

First and foremost, be aware of those around you. Question anything that appears to show a lack of conscience. When you worry about someone else's actions, don't hide that worry in a corner of your mind that never sees the light of reason. Never turn away. Examine each troublesome incident until it can be safely filed away in a folder labeled "dumb," or "only a mistake," or "inadvertent." If it doesn't fit in any of the safer categories, keep the incident in an open file that you visit every day. Keep it in the glaring light of active inspection until there is resolution. Again, never turn away from doubt. Never shrug your shoulders or turn your face away. Persist.

It is to the sociopath's advantage to appear normal, to blend in with society. To this end, they become masters of disguise. They lead a double life. The public sees what the sociopath wants them to see. The life he loves is hidden from their view. The sociopath's public persona has fewer boundaries than most of us. That's a major clue. Their private self knows no boundaries at all. Look closely for a lack of conscience. If you say to yourself, "I could never have done that to someone else," beware. Proceed with caution. If you find an overt disregard of morals, no guilt, no remorse, don't proceed at all. But do not look away. Don't rationalize. The results could be devastating. The end-game in the sociopath's wicked game is often emotionally crippling. Sometimes people die. Don't turn and look the other way. Don't pretend it isn't there. You will spend the rest of your life punishing yourself if you do not take a stand.

Question any oddity. Look for reason and sense within the answers. If the response is illogical, chances are you're listening to a lie. And know that just beneath the surface of that lie is the sociopath's real agenda. You are coming closer to his ulterior motive. The closer you come to understanding truth, the safer you will be.

Sociopaths are selfish by nature. They seldom engage in any activity that doesn't offer personal gain or recognition. Very often, in order to hide his selfish nature, he will engage in what seems selfless behavior. There's often a red flag there, something that seems not quite right, a little out of the ordinary. As example, the predator who sexually abuses children will often hide behind a facade of loving children. Look closely at illogical behavior where your child or any child is involved: the coach who does too much, the counselor who wants to see your child in his home, the playground supervisor who cannot keep his hands away from the children in his charge. The great majority of these, the coaches and counselors and playground supervisors, are good people and operate with the highest motives. But frighteningly, the sexual predator has learned to mimic their good behavior. But the signs are most often there. When you see something that doesn't seem quite right, it probably is not right. At minimum, each unusual action must be questioned. What appears to be a selfless gesture may turn out to be the snarling, clawed attack of the proverbial wolf in sheep's clothing. Once more, our best defense is awareness and willingness to question.

Chapter Four
HUNTER ON THE HUNT

The sociopath preys on others in a variety of ways and for a variety of reasons. His game is as variable as the weather. The only question is what he wants, what interests him, what deviant thrill he can derive from using you as the pawn in his never-ending game of self satisfaction. Often he doesn't really want what he takes from you. It is the very act of taking that thrills him. He will explore and exploit any crack in your armor to amuse himself. The conquest is all. The manipulation and control of whoever crosses his path is his sole reason for being. It is the reason he arises in the morning and what fuels his dreams at night. He is relentless in his pursuit. He never tires. He cannot accept "no" as a response to his inappropriate requests or demands. Interestingly, he particularly targets the soft hearted. They are easy prey, and he derives a macabre sense of satisfaction in damaging the trusting heart.

Perversely, the sociopath sees his own lack of conscience as strength. He does not understand morals, guilt, or remorse. He has no emotional attachment to others. He considers loyalty and gratitude as weakness.

The sociopath needs money to live. He needs money to further his games. He will take the easy money first, a few dollars here and there, lent and never repaid, then jump to taking whatever isn't guarded. No family member, spouse, close friend or business associate is immune from the financial scheming of the sociopath. It is an easy jump for him to help himself to another's checkbook and credit card, all without permission and all without remorse. From a few dollars loan to a request to a spouse to liquidate her funds is a simple path for the accomplished sociopath. He takes the same delight in emptying his child's piggy bank as he does in bankrupting a spouse. Only when the money trail is memory, when there are no future funds on the horizon, will the sociopath move on, leaving his victim broke, in debt, and often homeless. I know. I have walked that road.

The sociopath has an all-pervasive sense of entitlement, his path of self-gain sometimes leaving a criminal history. His record, if it is brought to light, may include theft, check fraud, identity theft, lawsuit abuse, insurance abuse, fraudulent loans, even robbery.

But money's not the main thing. While the money trail may be the easiest to discover and examine, it is important only in that it allows a certain lifestyle, allows the sociopath the freedom to continue his manipulation of others. Other people's money allows him the opportunity to spend his time mastering manipulation, to learn more sophisticated ways to damage others, to develop his cunning, to practice his perversions. The predator remembers what has and has not worked in the past. He applies this knowledge to the future. He begins to develop and refine techniques for manipulating his pawns. With passing time, these techniques become more sophisticated. With each success, his ways become more callused.

There is a second side to the predator's manipulation. Just as he delights in manipulating others, he also does his best to manipulate his environment, to make it safe, to let him hide from the light of knowledge. He will learn how the criminal system works. He will study that system to see how it can benefit him. He will tangle pursuit in red tape. He will lay a many layered smokescreen so he can go unnoticed. This is the framework the sociopath will use to continue his craft.

Chapter Five
LIES, LIES, AND MORE LIES

The lies generated by a sociopath are pathological by nature. A pathological liar can often be distinguished from an occasional liar by the shear volume of lies. This particular behavior appears to be driven by both obsession and compulsion. He has a compulsion to fool you. He is obsessed with seeing if he can. Because of this, even the simplest conversation will be studded with lies, half-truths, and misdirection. All of life becomes a game to see if he can fool you. Fortunately, the brazen lying often becomes bizarre. When it does that, it's easier to catch him in those lies. When he is caught in enough lies, the diagnosis becomes clear. When the diagnosis becomes clear, action can be taken. It must be taken, else he takes your self-respect and leaves you naked.

Within the sociopath's web of lies most often is a little truth, put there on purpose to hide the bigger lie. It may be something as inconsequential as the right day of the week or a time that can be checked. It's only there to add confusion, to make us jump to the idea that if any truth is there, he can't be telling lies. It is only a smoke screen, there to confuse us so the predator can continue his stalking uninterrupted and unobserved.

The sociopath uses lies to find more victims. Lying is often a fishing process, targeting the soft hearted. He gets his victims' cooperation with his smiling lies. But he goes too far. He reaches a point where his response to questioning leaves you unsatisfied, confused, weary of his false front. The oft-told lie wears thin and is seen for what it is. It is here you must not turn away. It is at this point where questioning must bombard him until he slips and gives himself away. To pull away, to turn the other cheek, would only give the predator a free pass for bigger impropriety. When you reach this point, get away. Protect yourself. Put distance between the predator and his pawn. And perhaps the hardest thing of all, get the authorities involved. It has been your often thankless job to discover his indecency. It has been a dark and lonely job. Turn the evidence over to the police. Let society shine the bright light of truth on what has happened. And thank the Lord you finally got away.

Chapter Six
THE CLOSET

I was visited with heartbreaking emotions when I first proposed to write this book. I didn't want needed details to again exploit any of his earlier victims. How, I wondered, could I teach people to avoid being victims in the future if I denied them the experience of the past? I strongly considered diluting the emotions, diluting the exploitation, diluting the impact on the individual. I was torn between wanting to protect others, and the natural tendency to protect myself from revisiting the terrible truths that wanted to seek me out and harm me once again. I wanted to hide. I wanted to dig a hole and pull myself in and never deal with the terror again. But if I truly wanted to help others avoid the traps set by a sociopath, I had to look straight into the face of the devil one more time. That sounds grand and altruistic, but admittedly, I had to use the truth to heal myself as well. If I looked away from evil, that evil would live inside me. If it continued to live inside me, I knew it would destroy me. I decided it was paramount to the truth, important to the reader, and absolutely necessary to my well-being to be open and frank and relentlessly honest. There were times I turned away from memories too painful to consider. But I always came back. I began again, in spite of the pain, and as the truth found its way into print, the pain was slowly replaced by pride. Surely the truth would be important to strangers who happened on this book. And surely, I began to see and understand, the truth would heal me. I prayed the truth might set me free.

I have minimized personal, identifying details. I have tried to protect the victim's identity. Still, I had to use enough detail that the behaviors of the sociopath could be put on display and recognized by the reader. Protecting identity while fully exposing techniques and tools used by the sociopath has been hard. I suspect I have erred in each direction. I hope I have not strayed too far in either misdirection. I ask the reader to look past the personal details of the sociopath's victims, and see the manipulator, the devil himself, at work. Observe closely. And being aware, beware. Observe the manipulations, lies, deceits, disguises, and deviant patterns of the sociopath. See the absence of conscience, emotional vacancy, total disregard and contempt for his victims. Imagine no loyalties, no concern or caring for anyone but himself. Imagine no restraints. Imagine, if you dare, the blank tablet inside the sociopath's mind.

Chapter Seven
THE PHONE CALL

I remember every detail of the phone call. I have perfect recall of the emotions that swept over me and threatened to pull me under. I recoiled from the fear that filled me. I remember my knees buckling and collapsing on the couch. The voice was telling me that Marvin was accused of being a pedophile, of seducing children. The sociopath beside me had finally gone too far. Children had talked and told, and while a dread nearly filled my soul, a small part of me felt a tiny tremor of hope. Now, perhaps, there might be a reckoning. But that call turned many lives upside down past understanding. The call brought horror out in the open and nearly robbed me of reason. I remember the voice on the phone being partially drowned out by a loud ringing noise in my ears, and how I was struggling to keep from passing out. I remember dropping the receiver onto the cushion next to me because my hand was trembling so violently that I could no longer grip the phone. I was so traumatized by the news that it took me a full minute to realize that the sobbing voice saying, "I'm so sorry, I didn't know", over and over again, was mine. The guilt and responsibility that I felt was crushing. My not knowing, my turning away from the truth, had protected Marvin. My turning a blind eye had let the sociopath beside me work his evil. It was my fault. My fault. My fault. Just as Marvin had intended.

I fell into his trap once more. My fault. My fault. But of course it wasn't. Marvin had turned the pointing finger toward everyone else in his ever expanding circle. He didn't have to give himself permission to be a pedophile. He was that already. It was his nature. But somewhere along the path, he had given himself permission to act on that base impulse. He had to give himself permission to act out against our most vulnerable, our children. He gave himself permission to rob children of their childhood, their innocence, their future. And all the while, he pointed the finger of blame in every direction but his own. Marvin did not have the ability to feel guilt. He told himself he was smarter than all the rest, that whatever happened to feed his desire was acceptable. If he could put blame on others, so much the better. The children's lives were forever changed. Despite the result of the investigation, they will bear their scars forever. But "my fault, my fault," I told myself, just as Marvin had intended.

The authorities began their investigations. Children as young as 8 years old were asked emotionally painful questions. They were led away from the darkness they had endured, but they were never completely cleansed. A corner of their mind stayed black. There was always and forever a place inside their head they visited in dreams, a place where the sociopath smiled and beckoned into the dark again. "My fault, my fault," they thought. "My fault, my fault," they cried, just as I had cried, and just as Marvin had intended all along.

Most of the children involved were initially escorted from their school classroom into a nearby conference room. How frightening that first interview must have been. They had to discuss this horrifying subject without warning. They had nowhere to hide, nowhere to escape. Again, just as Marvin had intended.

The entire community learned of this issue. The school became a haunting reminder of these events. The younger children whispered to each other. The older children spoke the horror out loud, and pointed at the victims as they passed by in the hall. The searching interviews were so psychologically scarring that some parents denied authorities access to their children and their stories. Once again, it was just as Marvin had intended.

All the interviews were documented in writing and videoed so no details would be forgotten. The amount of humiliation that these children, these victims, endured from self-accusation and self-doubt was nearly insurmountable. It was beyond heartbreaking. The investigation uncovered many secrets. I personally brought forward ten children, some as young as 8 years old, who told of Marvin's sexual improprieties. Did we find them all? There is a substantial amount of evidence indicating otherwise. The evidence suggests they will not be the last. The trauma was massive and far-reaching. The school and all the children who attended, the neighborhood and all the children that lived there, all of the people who loved those children, struggled. They struggled to emotionally survive these hideous discoveries. Some of them struggle still. Some will never get past this painful experience. Some will struggle all their lives. Some will die without resolution. Some will always have the monster in their minds.

Here are some of the techniques Marvin used to further his sexual exploits. He used his own, unsuspecting son to bait his trap, to lure other children into his depraved lair. The victims included not only children but also family members and friends of his only child.

He was well known in the neighborhood for extending frequent social invitations to his son's friends and playmates on his child's behalf. The idea for a party or gathering of children always came from Marvin, never from his son, though the opposite seemed the case. The number of parties was excessive, as was the number of children invited. A neighbor described his house as "having a steady stream of children parading through it, children pouring out the windows and doors. We thought of Marvin as a pied piper". In retrospect that was an apt analogy. Just as the Pied Piper led the mice of Hamlin to their death, so did this modern day piper lead the neighborhood children down a destructive path to a devil's playground. Under the guise of "Mr. Fun," he beckoned the children, and the children followed him home.

Nothing was off limits or too extreme for Marvin. After all, he'd say, it was all for the children's sake. Only in retrospect did his entertainment plans look unusual. Marvin borrowed the money to build an in-ground pool that took up the entire back yard. There was barely enough room for a walkway around the pool, hardly enough room to stand. Once completed, Marvin spent countless hours playing "Marco Polo", all day and late into the summer night, with any number of young boys. Marco Polo is a game of tag played under water. Marvin used the game to grasp a young boy's genitalia as his way of tagging. Those who pulled away became a part of his later defense. "Sure, I played Marco Polo with Marvin," they would say. "No, he never touched me there," they would add. "Well, maybe once, but that was a mistake. It never happened again." Those who giggled and allowed the touching became his prey. They were invited to sleepovers or even family camping trips. He loved to share his sleeping bag with boys. How could we not have seen? How could we have let such improprieties happen? That thought process, that self-doubt, was just as Marvin had intended. I repeat that phrase purposely. These things didn't just happen. They were not random events. Never. They were just as Marvin had intended.

Marvin developed a pattern of befriending the parents of his intended victims. He worked to gain their trust. Not only did that allow increased access to their children, it allowed him to begin to build his arsenal of silencing tools. His purpose was two-fold. He needed to conceal his hideous priorities, and he needed to silence those who knew about them.

Chapter Eight
SILENCING THE TRUTH

Marvin would befriend an entire family. Remember my earlier description? He was a consummate salesman, able to sell ice to Eskimos. He would shamelessly befriend unsuspecting parents of his intended victims. He would then use them for his own purpose. He could obtain their cooperation; manipulate them for a variety of reasons, either aggressive or protective, but always fitting in his secret agenda. He could play each family member for his own amusement, for his perverse pleasure, to further his own dark needs. He would look for "fractures" within the family structure itself. He would intentionally choose his child victim from those who came from a single parent home or whose' parents were divorced, even if there was a stepparent within their family. He viewed these scenarios as family division weaknesses that he could exploit.

He developed a pattern of preying on single mothers of male children, his interests being in her children, her money and her material assets. Once inserted in the mother's life, he would begin to look for ammunition for character assassination. He used any deviation from normal readily and easily. He would distort other people's mistakes to his own use. As an example, if a parent had used alcohol with Marvin, that mother or father was encouraged to have another drink, then another, until he had consumed too much. If that parent ever turned against him, he would claim they were a raging alcoholic or an addict, and they should not be believed over him. Marvin collected other's indiscretions like some people collect stamps. He kept them in a file in his mind, and when they were needed, he used these bits of information, sometimes disinformation, to paint the other as a trouble maker, or out to get him, or as an insult to anyone's intelligence. Later, as he had to defend himself against the accusations of child seduction, his explanations became more and more irrational, impossible to defend. But that was later, after the damage had been done, after lives were in peril, after Marvin's victims had risen out of the depths of his degradation and into the light of truth.

He would frequently seduce one of the parents into having an affair with him. On several occasions, he was able to seduce both parents. And then, of course, he had them in his grasp. When confronted with the accusations of child seduction, he would admit to the adult seduction, and say that the adult, one or either, had an axe to grind, that they were simply venting anger at their own sexual involvement. "Of course I didn't use the little boy," Marvin would say. "His mother is just pissed that she put out for me. You can't believe a woman scorned by her lover." Alternatively, he would threaten to reveal the affair to others in order to exercise control and intimidate anyone who threatened his agenda. If a child told his parents the truth about his improprieties, he would tell the parents that the child was confused, or had a behavior problem, or that he was incapable of committing such acts and the child was a liar, plain and simple. Even after the official investigation had shown Marvin for the predator he was, he tried to deflect accusations with these tactical lies. Before he was caught in his tangle of lies, he used an endless list of twisted truths, half-lies, and misdirections to confuse and further entrap the little boys. The list is almost endless. Among them were:

"Mr. Fun"

"I'll be your friend"

"No one understands you like I do"

"I'll always be here for you"

"We'll be a "forever family"

"Here's money"

"Here's stuff"

"I'll take you here"

"I'll take you there"

"I'll let you do things that your parents won't let you do and it'll be our little secret"

"We can have other secrets too, and no one will ever know".

Once he violated them, he then threatened them into silence with:

"If you tell I'll be mad at you"

"I'll tell them you're a liar and nobody will believe you"

"They'll believe me and no one will like you anymore"

"Your mom and dad won't love you anymore"

"No one will want you, not ever".

It was later discovered that some of the children delayed in telling what he had done to them to protect their friend, Marvin's son. He bought their silence with manipulative lies such as: "If you tell you'll get me into trouble. The police will put me in jail and then my son won't have a father. Do you really want to see your friend in a foster home? If that happens, you'll never see him again. Do you want such terrible things to happen just because we had a little private fun?" And very often, these little boys tried to hide their sexual involvement with Marvin to protect their innocent friend.

After two long years of multiple victims and recurrent abuse, some of the boys came forward, first telling their parents and then the authorities their heart-breaking stories of sexual abuse at the hands of a manipulative monster. Some of the children wept and begged that their friend not be placed in a foster home. And how many stories never saw the light? There are some today, grown men, who have never told and never will. They blame themselves, and hide that blame in a dark corner of their mind where the sun is not allowed to shine. Think of that. They blame themselves--- just as Marvin intended.

Chapter Nine
FALLEN

I have been a Registered Professional Nurse for thirty-three years, my entire adult life. I specialized in the area of psychiatric nursing for fifteen years and worked side by side with psychiatrists, psychologists, therapists and counselors in observing and analyzing human behavior. With the misfortune of knowing a sociopath on a very personal level for eighteen years, these tools were put to a very personal and ultimate test. I learned the only way anyone can protect himself from being a victim of a sociopath is by recognizing that deviant behavior for what it is. When I reached this understanding, I felt a force for good rise up within me. That was the driving force behind this book.

I want to share this understanding with you. I want these pages to contain the tools and armor that will let you escape the trap set by an evil predator. I want you to be able to avoid being the victim of a sociopath beside you.

I tried to hide behind generalities in the first half of this book. I think the warnings about deviant behavior are there. I think the descriptions of a sociopath's behavior are accurate. But hiding behind generalities mimicked the way I had turned from the truth when I was married to Marvin. In retrospect, I was not a wife, but a shield. Marriage protected Marvin from close scrutiny. It helped to keep him safe.

Early in the dating relationship, I wondered at Marvin's lack of sexual energy. I first thought it reassuring. When ardor faded very early in the marriage, I wondered at its lack, but looked away. I knew there was a great range of normal sexuality, and thought it unfortunate that my partner was the bottom of the scale. I looked for other virtues.

Marvin had charismatic charm. When I first met him he was 26, and seemingly wise beyond his years. He could state a lie with conviction or mix lies with truth until the mixture was accepted as fact. I wasn't the only one taken in by his lies. Many people were drawn into his web of deceit by his ability to articulate seeming absolute truth. We were drawn in by his charisma. He seemed faultless, perfect, and omniscient. I was blinded by the light and relished being there.

Marvin was never caught off guard. He was never at a loss for the nearly perfect words that would mold people and their perceptions. His mind was razor sharp, and he wielded his mind like a sword, cutting through objections. He molded and directed people and situations to whatever end would fulfill his needs. Nothing was for others. Nothing was for gain except his own. Nothing was sacred except his own ego. But we were the chosen ones, gathered around him in a protected cluster, secure and safe. The chosen ones! How wonderful it seemed at the time. How chilling it is to see it now. My God, the chosen ones! Chosen, used, manipulated, twisted into whatever he wanted us to be, lured into doing whatever he wanted us to do. And all for him. Always, just for him.

I lived on the fringe of what seemed a magic circle, unaware and awestruck, for several months. When he asked me to dinner, I jumped. How perfect, I thought. How grand. I was fascinated by this unusual young man. He inspired me with his intelligence and his charming demeanor. I was ready to love him, willing to take that great chance. We dated for several months, although the time together was both sparse and sporadic. Marvin was different, displaying no sense of physical or even emotional warmth. When he didn't call for a week or more, I would try to wean myself away from the idea of a personal connection with this enigmatic man. And then he would call again. I convinced myself that it was refreshing not to have to fight off sexual advances. I convinced myself that Marvin's intent was a plane above the sexual aggressiveness seen in so many men his age. I convinced myself that what Marvin presented was a purity that put him above the rest. Marvin was different, no question of that. But he was able to manipulate me and mold my feelings so that I accepted "different" as good. Not just good. Better. Best even. Marvin did that, all the while showing no need for emotional or physical warmth. And each time my emotions would falter, every time my feelings started to fade, Marvin would ask me out again, and every time the fascination would begin again.

Only in the blinding truth of retrospection did his plan unfold so I could see it. Marvin didn't love me. He was incapable of that emotion. He needed me to protect his image, to bolster his facade of secure heterosexuality. That's why he always put his best foot forward. That's why he tried to impress me. That's why he did what he did with me and with every one of us.

The appearance of heterosexuality allowed him to hide in the safest hiding place of all, in plain sight. But I didn't know that when I married him. I had fallen in love. That was all that mattered.

Chapter Ten
BEN

Three months into our dating relationship, came a pounding at the door. In bounds a young man named Ben, calling Marvin "dad". "Dad?" Until Ben's appearance, I hadn't heard mention of his existence, which in and of itself was certainly odd and spoke volumes. Marvin was 26 and Ben was 18, so I knew there wasn't a biological connection.

Ben appeared to be this massive amount of runaway energy in human form; like an out-of-control speeding train with a predicted wreck in the near future. He bounded through the doorway, and into the apartment, darting from one location to another, pacing around the furniture, looking at everything but seeing nothing. He finally landed in front of me, all wild-eyed, just long enough to say "hello," while still remaining in a state of perpetual motion by rocking on the soles of his feet. His excessive energy was palpable, and miserable to both witness and experience. His presence was toxic and affected living things in its path. I could feel my own pulse begin to race and my blood pressure rise. I had to consciously regain my composure so that I wasn't so overwhelmed by his nearness. The nurse in me equated this to be the worst case scenario of out-of-control hyperactivity that I had ever seen. One that was obvious and raging, one that certainly would benefit from pharmacological intervention. I was moved by Ben's visible suffering from this massive state of imbalance. A condition that could have been tempered with proper care. I felt pity for Ben.

Marvin's response to Ben's unannounced appearance was to rush Ben back out the door just as suddenly as he had appeared, as if he didn't want the two of us to meet.

After Ben's hasty departure, Marvin told me very little about who Ben was or about his life with him. His silence on the subject was all but deafening. When Marvin did tell me about Ben, it was in this strangely composed, casual manner. Instead of sensing warmth or nurturing, I sensed coldness and indifference, as if he were emotionally detached. At the time, I wondered if his mind was racing in an effort to choose just the right information and just the right words for the occasion. I observed him closely to see how he would proceed with his explanations.

In a detached manner he told me that when he was 21, he had adopted Ben who was 12 at the time. He casually related that he raised Ben, by himself, until just recently, when Ben turned 18 and moved out. He mentioned only two other details about Ben. That Ben had "special needs" that were documented as behavior problems, and that until the age of 14, Ben spent most of his time watching cartoons while wearing nothing but his underwear. He guarded everything else about his life with Ben. He never spoke of Ben again, as if Ben never existed.

Marvin made sure that while Ben was in his care that he never left him alone with anyone. Marvin claimed it was so that he could monitor his physical and emotional needs, but in retrospect it was to keep Ben from telling. When Ben moved out at the age of 18, Marvin kept him away from family. It appeared that Ben had been ejected and then discarded. Ben moved away to another state and had very minimal contact with his "dad."

Yes I harbored an uneasiness that Marvin was hiding information about his time spent with Ben, but it appeared that I was the only one with these sentiments regarding this bizarre arrangement. Apparently the adoption agency that was involved in Ben's adoption felt this was an appropriate placement for him. So I convinced myself that this uneasiness I experienced was not a product of active intuition, but instead a product of over-active imagination. I regret I made these rationalizations.

Why weren't Marvin's parents suspicious of this bizarre relationship? I suspect they were coached to believe that Marvin had performed a selfless act, that he had made a great sacrifice. They were proud of their son. And I admit, I looked past the obvious until years later, when the accusations had been made and huge parts of the puzzle fell into place. I gave Marvin the benefit of the doubt. I took the easy path and looked away. How difficult that is to say. I saw Ben one time, and looked away. I will regret that all my life.

Now in the light of retrospection, coupled with the facts about Marvin's recognized patterns of behaviors; if it is true that history repeats itself, here is my educated assumption regarding the truth about Ben:

I believe that at the young age of 21, this sociopath was already so cunning, so sophisticated, that he decided to adopt a victim. Ben would become his intended possession. Marvin would now "own" Ben. Marvin would choose Ben carefully. His physical appearance, his age, his gender, were all considerations. It's a documented fact that the criminal penalties for pedophiles are more severe for molesting children under the age of 12. Ben was no longer under the age of 12.

Ben's documented behavior problems were a definite bonus in his sinister plan. If Ben were to ever break Marvin's code of silence, Marvin would use this information to assassinate Ben's character. "Who would believe a screwed-up kid over an upstanding adult", Marvin could later proclaim. This is why Marvin chose to broadcast this specific detail to others, just to pave the way for him to play this card in the future, should he ever decide to do so.

I believe that Ben was on medication for hyperactivity before he was placed in Marvin's care. I also believe that Ben was taken off this medication by Marvin. After all, medication costs money. And the regular trips to the doctor to monitor these medications could now be avoided. He surely didn't want Ben to meet with any doctor. Something else might be uncovered, like the truth. Yes, I believe that Marvin let Ben suffer in silence for his own personal gain and told those who inquired that Ben was over-medicated and that Marvin's actions were really a rescue effort on his part.

Marvin's adoption of Ben also yielded him an additional monthly income from the State. Funds that contained an increase in its amount due to Ben's documented behavior issues. It was as if Marvin was getting paid to "own" Ben.

Yes, Marvin had it all figured out. What better way to keep a victim "under your thumb" to control them, than to keep them under your roof and under your wing. Silencing Tools.

As for the odd mentioning of Ben wearing nothing but his underwear; this was most probably done to broadcast an example of Ben's inappropriateness and also a twisted opportunity for Marvin to conjure up another stimulating mental image of Ben.

Ben was ejected from Marvin's home and his life, when Ben turned 18, when the monthly checks from the State ceased. Now Ben was no longer "useful". He was surely a loose cannon. Ben moved to another state and rarely contacted Marvin.

While Marvin was a fugitive from justice, with the authorities searching for his whereabouts, Marvin traveled to the state where Ben resided, to meet with him. A special farewell, with threatening overtones to hopefully silence Ben permanently should authorities discover his existence and locate him for questioning. A parting gift especially designed for Ben.

I never saw or heard of Ben again. But I did not look away from Ben this time. This time I told.

Chapter Eleven
CONSTANT COMPANIONS

I noticed that people constantly surrounded Marvin. He didn't seem to need a private time. Male friends routinely drove from an hour and a half away to see him. Someone always spent the weekend with him.

I discovered through the course of the next eighteen years that every person on his "friend list" was also on his seduction list. He preferred males, but used women as well. Gender was irrelevant. Sex was a game with intercourse the prize. An orgasm was something he could take from you. That's all that mattered. The more chaos he could create when seducing someone, the more he enjoyed himself. And he was persistent. Only those who repeatedly refused his advances would survive this outcome.

Chapter Twelve
THE NON-INTIMATE RELATIONSHIP

The only intimacy Marvin and I shared in the first four months of our relationship was a hurried peck on the lips. I was concerned by lack of chemistry and physical attraction. I thought about ending the relationship and cutting my losses. Marvin sensed this, and instigated intimacy. That's not a good word. It was a completed sexual act, but it was not intimate. Marvin exhibited no signs of passion. It was as if he were struggling to perform. But it reassured me that I was loved. It was enough to make me close my eyes to his sexual shortcomings. It allayed my fears enough that I married Marvin. I was happy. Marvin was shielded. What a strange relationship. What lies.

Now the reasons are clear. Marvin was not physically attracted to any female. I doubt there was any sense of giving in having sex with men. He used the sex act solely as a means of conquest. It was a source of control and power purely for the sake of his amusement. After seven years of a manipulative marriage, we were divorced. I needed more from life and Marvin surely was tired of pretending he could be a proper husband. But I remained a friend he could call and brag to and boast about his business successes. We had moved a distance apart, and now our communication was by telephone. He would call me several times a month to boast about his latest business venture or the new contract that he was able to win. He delighted in telling me the details of his latest business conquest.

Marvin was a sales representative for a small but specialized company. He was able, with great ease and little effort, to acquire a sizable contract nearly every month. He would set up meeting with the intended client, show up in his recently "detailed" BMW, wearing a $1,000 suit, and chauffeur that client to a fine restaurant. Most often he would get the contract he sought. He lived well on the companies' credit card.

Later, after the fall, it became apparent how Marvin got his way. He had sexually seduced his boss, and shortly after that, seduced his boss's wife. Less than a year after those conquests, his base salary was raised from $35,000 to $100,000 a year. His commissions doubled and sometimes tripled his income.

Marvin seduced several co-workers and clients. His list of conquests was growing. He now had a number of people who would do his bidding, and never be able to undo what had been done. Being sexually conquered, they could be used for a lifetime.

Chapter Thirteen
PENNY

Six months after we were divorced, Marvin invited me to his wedding. He was marrying his neighbor, Penny. When they first met, she was married and had three young boys, ages 8, 10, and 12. Marvin had seduced her and convinced her to file for divorce from her husband of twenty years. Marvin suggested an attorney for her to use, one that he selected on her behalf. One with a merciless reputation and the vicious qualities of a Pit Bull, the kind of qualities that he himself admired. He would be sure to carefully observe this lawyer's tactics and techniques, like a student would a mentor. These "private lessons" would be valuable to him, and of course, paid for on someone else's dime. This lawyer would render Penny's husband nearly destitute. Broke, most of his acquired assets lost in this divorce that was overseen and coached by a sociopath. Penny's husband was evicted from his home of twenty years, as his wife and three children went to live in the house next door.

Marvin married Penny two weeks later, and the following week a "For Sale" sign went up in front of Penny's old house. In a matter of weeks, it sold at $85,000. After twenty long years of house payments this house was just recently paid off. Now all that money was Marvin's.

Along with the sale of her house he manipulated Penny into selling her other assets; antique furniture, and a paid for truck. Within a four month period of time, Penny's paid for house, furniture, and vehicle were all gone. And so was the money from the sale of her items.

Now that Penny was cash broke and without assets, he would devise another plan to open up other opportunities for him to take from her. He was like a vampire draining the last available drop of blood from his victim. He applied for numerous credit cards via the mail, using each card for the maximum amount of available credit. He forged Penny's signature on the applications, with him only a secondary cardholder. Thus, he had complete use of these many credit cards, and no fiscal responsibility.

Marvin accessed Penny's Credit Union account, and found that he could withdraw up to $6,000. He received that check in the mail just one week after forging the application to withdraw. Somehow, he was able to cash that check.

Marvin would begin to use the credit cards that he had applied for; they were coming in the mail at a rapid rate. He hurriedly went about the task of using them to charge items up to their maximum credit limit. So on it continued for Penny, with his "what's yours is mine and what's mine is mine" type attitude in full operation. This would be the case until he could squeeze her completely dry, and then he planned to discard her.

Now that the scheme to max-out the credit cards was well on its way, he would look for other things that he could take from Penny. He would focus his devious attention on the one thing left to take from her, her children.

Two months after Marvin put all of Penny's funds in his own name, two of her children came to Penny and told her that they were being made to "do things" with their new stepfather. They gave their mother graphic details of what had occurred in her absence. The youngest child, Nick, then 8 years old, denied any such encounters of his own. When Marvin arrived home, Penny immediately confronted him.

Marvin flew into a rage, a rage inspired strictly for the sake of theatrics. He really wasn't angry, nor was he sorry. He could have cared less about his victims state of suffering, it was all about him. Marvin was afraid because he had gotten caught. He wasn't in fear of any legal consequences because he would see to it that there were none, one way or another; he was smarter than "the system". What he was in fear of, and the last thing that he would allow to happen, would be for his activities to be interrupted. Marvin pounced on the opportunity at hand; to use the very scenario that presented itself as an excuse to outwardly terrorize this family, Penny and the children being alone with him in the house. He stormed about the house, raging and pounding on walls and destroying some of the children's toys, their beloved PlayStation and other belongings. Marvin screamed that they were "all a bunch of losers and ingrates" and that "without him they were nothing", making sure that everyone within the confines of the house would hear its echoes. He yelled that the children were "retarded" and that their mother was "insane" and that they were all "liars and he would prove it". Now, he intentionally lowered his voice, so only Penny could hear what was to follow.

With an icy-cold glare Marvin looked her directly in the eyes and hissed "who would believe someone who's insane? They'll believe me." Penny's blood ran cold. She knew what he was alluding too. She had been diagnosed years ago with bipolar disorder and was taking prescribed medication for this condition. Then Marvin announced that he would be divorcing her; and as a reminder that all her assets and money were gone he added "and where ya gonna go with your brats you stupid bitch?"

An even more sinister plan occurred to Marvin. "I'll prove you're an unfit mother and gain custody of your children." "Go take some more of your pills bitch, you're gonna need it." It was as if the devil himself was whispering in Marvin's ear as to what to say. And that's precisely what Penny did, as if she were hypnotized.

The very thought of this malignant monster gaining possession of her children generated a psychological and emotional meltdown in Penny. She could not bear the thought of what she was about to have to endure. Penny snapped. Void of all rational thought and as if she were following Marvin's command, Penny went into the bathroom medicine cabinet, got her bottle of pills, and swallowed what remained in the bottle in front of Marvin. He didn't jump into action and try to stop Penny. Instead, he stood by and watched her. Marvin felt this intense jolt of power that he had never experienced before, a total unharnessed rush of adrenaline. Could he have become so adept at manipulating people and events that he could get them to obey such life-altering commands? He felt all-powerful. He would savor the image of this moment forever.

Marvin didn't respond by calling 911 to report an overdose to summon an ambulance for Penny. He didn't dial for help to try to save her life; instead he simply glared at her with contempt. Penny knew about the children now, but she hadn't yet had the opportunity to tell anyone. If Penny did die she wouldn't be able to tell, ever. And the fact that she did it to herself, all the better! Within the next fifteen minutes, Penny regained enough rational thought to call for her own ambulance. She was treated and released from the hospital several hours after she arrived.

Before Penny awoke the next morning, Marvin left the house to begin damage control. He chose an attorney, the same aggressive, Pit Bull, take no prisoners, lawyer he had used before. Marvin liked his style. And he also thought that he would more than likely get some sort of preferential treatment since he was a repeat customer. Marvin was right about that. And he always made sure to remind his attorney just what a valuable client he was. Marvin had just awarded his attorney two cases that morning; one, the divorce from Penny; and the other, a child custody case, because he was filing to keep Nick, as he had promised Penny.

Marvin filed whatever had to be done to keep Nick, and filed for divorce from Penny. He had her money. He was taking her child. Now he needed to discredit her testimony if she pursued a child abuse case. Four days after filing these two cases, Marvin told Penny to get out and take her two brats with her. Only two. He told her he was keeping Nick. Somehow, he orchestrated that. Marvin made it happen. He kept Nick because Nick didn't tell. Nick had denied any indecencies with Marvin. I don't know how Marvin managed that. I believe he filled Nick with cunning lies.

I believe that somehow Marvin convinced Nick that he was better off with him. I suspect he told him that being an only child would provide him with more than he would have with Penny. He wouldn't have to share; everything would be just for him. Marvin poisoned Nick with lies about his family. He bribed the boy with "stuff." He had a powerful hold on this 8 year old child.

Penny was emotionally battered to the point she left the house with her two older boys, leaving Nick alone with a child-molesting sociopath. He convinced a small circle around him that Penny was insane, and the older son's were confused because of their mother's insanity. Nick was young enough not to have been infected with his mother's madness, Marvin maintained. And certainly Nick's consistent denials that there had been improprieties gave Marvin a thick smoke screen to hide behind. Nick was questioned by many people, but stayed with his story of innocence. Marvin, with Nick's help, convinced the legal system that keeping Nick, at least temporarily, was for the best, and he was awarded temporary custody of the young boy.

Again I gave "the system" the benefit of the doubt. I had to believe that the authorities had investigated the situation thoroughly before awarding custody of a child to a man who was not his father.

I'm sure that Penny's suicide attempt had a lot to do with the outcome. He painted Penny as unstable, which of course she was. He neglected to mention that he had been the one to convince her to take more medicine; that he had badgered her with, "Take more of your pills, bitch," until she snapped and did just that. Marvin broadcasted Penny's bipolar diagnosis to all his acquaintances, and implied that the children likely would have starved if he had not taken over the cooking in the home. When he was asked why he filed for custody of only Nick instead of all three children, Marvin said that he and Nick had a special bond. "Nick loves me and needs me," Marvin said. "That little boy needs me and he thinks I hung the moon."

Marvin had custody of Nick for the next five months. I saw them together at a school function once during that time. Nick was draped across Marvin's lap, his head resting on his stepfather's chest. The boy reached up and put his arms around the older man's neck. His little voice was almost dreamy as he cooed, "I really love you, daddy." Nick was not yet nine.

Chapter Fourteen
PENNY'S STRUGGLE

The days ahead for Penny were a monumental struggle. This marriage had lasted only eight months but left her life in ruins. She had to wonder if she would ever get her son back from this monster. She didn't know if she would be able to gather up the broken pieces of her life. She had no way of knowing if she could repair the damage to her reputation, to her family, to her concept of self. She didn't know if her children would heal from the assault by this monstrous human being, or if they'd ever get their little brother back. She had a divorce pending and no funds for legal counsel. She was squeezed dry, and withered, and had no place to turn. She was fighting a calculating evil, and the system didn't seem to want to help her.

Two months after Marvin and Penny separated; I received a call from Marvin asking me to be a character witness for him at Nick's custody hearing. I was nauseated by the request, and very nearly vomited. For the first time, I shook off the lethargy that I thought had protected me, and that I often hid behind. I didn't fold and look away from danger. I told him he should be ashamed, trying to take a little boy from his mother. I asked him how he would feel if someone tried to do that to him. His answer was a furious, spitting, surge of anger. "That bitch is trying to put me in jail!" Nothing more. No rational explanation. No attempt to sway me with facts. Just, "that bitch is trying to put me in jail." "Good," I thought to myself, but only told him I wouldn't help. Finally I had faced Marvin. Finally I had mustered the courage to deny him something he wanted. A rush of satisfaction flowed through me and painted my cheeks and made me catch my breath. Finally!

As soon as Marvin had assumed custody of Nick, Penny's father requested a meeting. He begged Marvin to return his grandson to his daughter. He confronted Marvin about selling all of Penny's possessions and spending the money on himself. Marvin held the meeting in his kitchen, and prepared for it by placing a tape recorder behind the refrigerator to record what was said. He wanted to catch the old man in an impropriety, something he could use against him if he needed. He didn't find anything, but he later related that he listened to the recording often, laughing at the old man begging for the return of his grandson.

I don't understand the why's and wherefore's, but Marvin managed to have his marriage to Penny annulled. It meant no child support, no alimony, and Penny remained broke while Marvin's financial future was unscathed. He and his lawyer convinced the court that the child molestation charges were the fantasy of a woman scorned, and were not valid. Marvin told us that the molestation charges were dropped because he demanded to take a polygraph, and the results showed that he was telling the truth, that he was not abusing children. I strongly suspect that this polygraph test never happened. I have heard that there are sociopaths who have such perfect control over their reactions that they can pass a polygraph test in spite of being guilty. How can this be? It's simple enough. Sociopaths are so bereft of conscience that emotions are not a factor. They see whatever they do as right and proper. Their pulse and blood pressure will not rise in the absence of guilt.

Marvin further insinuated that the reason Nick was remanded to his mother's care was that his lawyer was dyslexic, had trouble with paperwork, and was late in filing a key document. Marvin claimed he was incompetent. He complained that he had paid some $30,000 in legal fees in a custody case that had gone against him, and now the lawyer "owes me big time."

Martin in fact had used Penny's money to fight her in Nick's custody battle. He had opened a secret bank account while still married, where he deposited some of his takings from her. He used this money to try to take Nick from Penny.

Penny's father was worried about his daughter, and tried to file a civil suit to regain some of his daughter's stolen finances. Marvin got more credit cards, maxed them out buying and borrowing as much as he could with them, and then filed bankruptcy. He was able to keep $90,000 in newly purchased assets. He hired an accountant to repair his credit scores, and was able to obtain a new stack of credit cards. Nothing was left for Penny. The civil suit was dropped.

Chapter Fifteen
MALIGNANT

Marvin continued his whirlwind sociopathic games. He continued his non-stop seductions. He would take all he could from his prey, suck them dry of money, favors, and dignity. He was contemptuous of all his victims. He thought them all inferior, only useful for what he could take from them. He felt entitled, superior in every way. Each manipulation provided him with a new adrenaline rush.

One afternoon he purchased a book titled, How To Cast Spells. He proudly displayed it on his coffee-table . I doubt he had ever read a complete book, so this was out of character. There were no other books in his house. I am sure of that. But How To Cast Spells was there for all of us to see. Marvin saw the curiosity on my face as I stared at the book one afternoon and volunteered, "I can make things happen to people just by thinking them." He then told me of a teacher he had hated as a kid. Alone in bed one night, he actively wished the teacher harm. The next day the teacher's family were all killed in an automobile accident. Marvin smiled when he told me that story. There was an evil sneer on his face as he added, "believe it. It is true." I thought then and still believe that Marvin had begun his descent into madness.

Marvin spent hours at his office computer every day, searching gay man-boy websites. Through an international website, he found a gay male twenty years his junior, who lived in Russia. This boy spoke broken English and was poor. He didn't own a computer but would walk to a library to access the use of one. In Russia at that time, it was illegal to engage in any homosexual activities. Although it was punishable by a mandatory prison term, Marvin convinced the boy to maintain contact, and planned to sponsor the boy and send him enough money to get a visa and come to the States to live with him. What a perfect victim. If he did not comply with Marvin's demands, he could be left alone in a foreign land. He would have no shelter, and would barely be able to communicate. I don't know why the plan failed. I do know that failure was a monumental gift for the Russian boy. This failed plan and others like it were discovered after the fact by criminal investigators. I shudder when I think of the expansion of Marvin's capabilities allowed by a computer. Now he had the whole world at his fingertips. He could expand his deviant search around the globe. He could find victims anywhere.

Chapter Sixteen
EDDIE

It was years after the fact that I found out about Eddie. An investigator looking into Marvin's past interviewed me, and in the process of that interview, told me about the 8 year old boy. The story nearly mirrored Ben's, but had a different ending. Once again, Marvin tried the adoption process. He used his computer to view photos and profiles of many candidates. He cruised electronically, searching posted information and imagining possibilities. He looked for what he had with Ben: a boy with emotional disabilities that would make a prospective couple look elsewhere, and that made adoption by a single male more feasible.

His brazen schemes were more refined, more cunning. Marvin found a way to make himself sound reasonable, at least in a computer print-out. He developed patterns of behavior from sifting through his past. He found what hadn't worked, and threw those ideas out. He looked at the things that had worked, and honed his skills using those techniques.

He developed plans for his future entertainment, for a future filled with Bens and Pennys and multiple seductions and molestations. The hunt was more protected when done with a computer, but the thrill of the chase wasn't satisfied electronically. The computer was fine for a search, but he needed live people for his active seduction. He needed a child from another state so it would be highly unlikely that his past would come to bear. Ben had to remain undiscovered if Marvin was to adopt again.

He hoped all information regarding his documented past would slip through the cracks in the system. There were no trials, no time in prison, no court decisions that went against him. All that showed in written record was the "bit of bother with that bitch Penny and her two brats." The charges had been dropped in that case, but Marvin did not want anyone to connect events in his past with his plans for here and now. So when his computer search found Eddie, Marvin set his evil sights on him. He would replace Ben with Eddie.

Eddie was an 8 year old boy with documented behavior problems. He lived in a foster home in another state. Eight years old was good for Marvin. A little boy that age was easier to convince and to control; easier to manipulate and bend to his private pleasure. Marvin was certain he could handle an 8 year old. He was more confident now of manipulating both the adoptive system and the courts. It had worked before, he thought, and he had learned a lot since then.

The adoption agency did not learn of Ben. They told Marvin they would give him Eddie for a trial period, but first wanted them to spend just one night together as a test of compatibility, and of Marvin's ability to handle a hyperactive child. Eddie's hyperactivity was equally as bad as Ben's had been, but the child was well controlled on medication. Marvin saw no problem there. Eddie was beside himself with excitement. The thought of someone wanting to adopt him filled his heart with hope. As they drove away, he waved goodbye to the other children, aware that he was one of the lucky ones. Then he turned his attention to Marvin, who told him of the fun they would have at an amusement park, and at supper, and getting to know each other when they spent the night together. Marvin said they could eat anywhere that Eddie wanted. The little boy's mind was filled with dreams, and he grinned from ear to ear.

When they reached the theme park, Eddie leapt out and raced to the entrance. It was a paradise, something he had imagined but never thought he would see. He spent the day taking it all in; the rides, the games, the food. Finally his senses were on overload, and he was exhausted. Marvin insisted on one more indulgence. They stopped on the way to the hotel for ice cream. It was another first in a day of firsts. Eddie had his fill of ice cream. That day was a dream come true. His fill of ice cream! Imagine!

With a belly full of ice cream and a mind filled with wonder, Eddie arrived at the hotel. Marvin showered while Eddie watched television, then told Eddie to shower as well. Marvin, covered with just a towel, watched Eddie closely as the boy disrobed. He watched just as closely as Eddie dried himself and started to put on pajamas. Marvin took off his towel, climbed into the bed naked, and told Eddie that it was so much more comfortable to sleep "in the raw." Marvin patted the place beside him and smiled. "Come on, Eddie. We'll need a good night's sleep before tomorrow's fun."

The hours that followed were worse than any nightmare Eddie had known or imagined. He found the Boogey Man really did exist. Each time in the past he had dreamt of him, the Boogey Man was gone when he woke up in the morning. This time he was here to stay, and he wanted to keep Eddie forever.

Eddie went berserk. He flew out from under the covers, shaking and crying. He tried to cover his nakedness with one hand, pointed the other at Marvin and cried, "Take me back. Take me back right now." This 8 year old turned his back on a dream he had held since he could remember. He rejected the dream of a place of his own, and demanded that Marvin take him back to the foster home. His screaming was so loud that Marvin had no choice.

On the trip back, Marvin had to figure out an excuse for bringing the boy back in the early morning. He decided on the story that Eddie's hyperactivity had gone out of control and he was unable to control the child. Then Marvin turned his full attention on the little boy crying in the back seat of the car. He couldn't kill him, although that was within his limitations. People knew where the boy was and who he was with. He'd never get away with that. Marvin decided that he had to frighten Eddie so badly that the child would be afraid to tell.

During the entire length of the ride back to the foster home, he spat hurtful and scarring things to Eddie. He was relentless and cruel wanting to inflict these images onto Eddie's psyche and his heart. This monster was far more frightening and cruel than any of the monsters that resided in Eddies worst nightmares, as Marvin unleashed all his verbal ammunition in his arsenal on this 8 year old little boy. He told Eddie that no one would believe him. He said he would tell the people at the foster home that Eddie was a liar, and that no one would like him anymore. Marvin told this little boy that once the word got out about his lying, no one would want him. "You'll never be adopted," he said. "You will live, unwanted, in a foster home forever."

When Marvin dropped Eddie off at the foster home he gave his explanation of being unable to control the boy's hyperactivity, and drove away. And Eddie told. This little 8 year old depicting a mountain of courage, described Marvin's attempt at molestation, and the staff believed him. As protocol required, they reported the incident to Child Protective Services. They in turn reported it to the police. After interviewing Eddie and investigating the circumstances, the police filed child molestation charges against Marvin. Somehow, Marvin got away unscathed.

Chapter Seventeen
JOSEPH

Sometime after Marvin and I were divorced, I married again, this time to a man with three young sons, ages 8, 10, and 12. The boys lived with their biological mother, but spent weekends, some holidays, and summer vacations with their father and with me. Motherhood is always hard. Instant step-mothering must be one of the most difficult jobs there is. Three months after my marriage, I received a call from Marvin telling me he had adopted a child, a 10 year old boy named Joseph. I hadn't heard of this before, and was shocked. I knew of the charges in Penny's case, but also knew the charges had been dropped. The authorities had approved Ben's adoption, and nothing unusual had surfaced yet. There was nothing yet that a rational mind could capture, no concrete evidence of Marvin's pedophilia. But my emotional self was beginning to over-ride my rational being. It wanted me to look beneath the surface and find what might be there.

I hesitate to tell you what happened next, but I received a message in my mind from somewhere outside my intuition. It was telepathic. It said, "Things are not what they appear to be." That was all. "Things are not what they appear to be." I was flooded with an overwhelming sense that I needed to be vigilant, that

Joseph was in danger. The experience took my breath away.

I wanted nothing more to do with Marvin. I wanted to push him as far away from me as I could. Instead, I had just been "requested" to do the opposite. I felt I had to do what I could to protect Joseph; that I had to encourage his presence in my life. That persistent voice from somewhere outside of my mind was telling me to do what I could to protect someone else's child. I had to try, but I was filled with dread.

I took this opportunity to have a discussion with the boys, the one about "telling" if someone ever tried to touch them on their "privates" without their permission, all the while tailoring the information so young boys could comprehend the danger. They promised me at that kitchen table, that not only would they tell, but that they would "beat the person up." They showed me how, rushing around the kitchen demonstrating moves they'd learned from Power Rangers cartoons. I laughed, but made them promise they would tell.

Marvin was persistent. He called me often, checking on me and saying "you two must need a break from those three rambunctious boys. How about I babysit them for a couple of days. Joseph would enjoy their company."

I told him we never felt the need for a babysitter that the children weren't with us very often so our time together as a family was important. Marvin never gave up asking, reminding me he wanted my boys to spend the weekend "for Joseph's sake".

Instead, I invited Joseph to come over to our place to play with the boys, sometimes for the weekend. At first, Marvin declined the offer. He didn't want to leave Joseph alone with anyone for fear that he would tell. However, one day he agreed to let Joseph come spend the night. He allowed this twice. Both times he called and spoke at length to Joseph. I can only assume he was making sure that Joseph would not tell.

Now when Marvin would call, I would intentionally guide him off the subject of himself, and onto Joseph. I had to be careful to limit my questions by picking and choosing which ones appeared to need my additional attention; the ones where "red flags" would wave. And the questions themselves had to be hidden in the discussion, as if I weren't questioning at all but just making conversation, all the while weaving the subject I wanted to know more about into its mix. It was critically important that he not become suspicious of me for fear this would cause him to become either guarded or cut me off all together. I had to play dumb, to appear non-threatening to his activities. Joseph depended on me to perfect this personal dance that was so delicate between his adoptive father and myself. This was so important and so fragile that it frightened me, and I wasn't up against any normal human being, I was up against a cunning monster. I knew the consequences that even one slight misstep on my part meant for his victims. Two could play at this manipulation game. Mine a force for good, his a force for evil. So I continued to encourage conversation with the Devil.

During the course of one of our telephone talks, he told me that he'd borrowed $35,000 from the bank so he could install an in-ground pool in his back yard for Joseph. I wondered aloud if there was room. Marvin assured me it would fit. It left no room for Joseph to play, but Marvin felt it would improve Joseph's social contacts. He was designing the devil's playground. And that's what it became.

Marvin had become "Mr. Fun". He proclaimed this aloud in front of the children. He would allow them to do anything they wanted while they were at his house. He even encouraged them to watch pornographic movies on the television in his family room. He plied the older boys with alcohol and marijuana. He was getting bolder, and he was taking chances. He was nearly caught several times. One time a boy told his parents he smelled pot at Marvin's house. Another time a mother found a joint in her son's pocket. Another boy, younger, told his mother he wanted to direct porno films when he grew up.

The underwater groping under the guise of "Marco Polo" became endemic. Marvin always claimed he couldn't see underwater, or, "you moved. I didn't mean to touch you there." But Marvin wanted even more. He infiltrated Joseph's school, and volunteered to coach basketball.

Marvin had never played a game of basketball. He didn't even know the rules. This didn't pose a problem. He looked up what he needed, and became the after-school basketball coach. The boys looked up to him and respected him; they called him coach. And of course these boys would get sleepover invitations to Marvin's house along with all the others.

Conveniently, the shower-head nozzle In Joseph's bathroom quit working. Marvin told Joseph that he and any overnight guests would have to shower in Marvin's bathroom, a bathroom that adjoined the master bedroom. He walked in on whoever was using the shower, never apologized, but always found a reason to linger. Many of the boys complained to

Joseph, and told him it was weird. What they didn't know was that Marvin had installed a video camera that filmed the naked boys while they were showering. He replayed these films for his twisted viewing pleasure on the rare nights he was alone.

After spending the night with Joseph, a 10 year old boy named Stuart told his mother that Joseph's dad had "touched" him. Marvin's explanation to this single mother was that he was helping Stuart apply medicated cream to his jock itch. He then seduced her to silence her suspicions.

An 11 year old boy Curtis told his mother that Joseph's dad had "touched his wiener". Marvin's explanation was that they were cooking hot dogs on the grill and the joke related to that. He said it was all a misunderstanding. Curtis refused to discuss this incident again, not with his friends, not with his parents, and not later with the authorities. He didn't deny it happened. He just refused to discuss it or acknowledge that it happened. He wanted it to go away.

Marvin gained access to my stepchildren through their biological mother. Joseph called her and asked if the boys could spend the weekend at his house. She was reluctant, since she had never met Joseph's father. Marvin got on the phone and persuaded her. He told her he had bought season passes to a well-known amusement park in the area, he would take them there, if not this weekend, any time they wanted. He said that he would pick them up and bring them home on Sunday. What time they spent at his house, they could play in his swimming pool. He added that he would supervise them responsibly. He had by-passed me and gained access to my children. That weekend, he sexually molested them. It was my fault! My fault! As they had promised me they would, they told their mother and she called me.

After the phone call had ended, I picked myself up, put on my shoes and my "war face". My husband asked me where I was going, I replied "I'm going over there to kill Marvin, to snap his neck with my bare hands, or die trying. And then I'm taking Joseph." My husband stopped me. He made me promise to let the authorities handle it. And that they would rescue Joseph as soon as we filed charges against Marvin. We both agreed at this time that we would tell the authorities that we would care for Joseph from this point forward, not to return him to the foster home. That we desired and would request to be his family. We briefly discussed the problem, then informed Child Protective Services. New charges were filed within the next forty-five minutes.

Our youngest boy, Pauly, who was 9 at the time that he was molested, acquired a sudden and odd desire to begin buying pocket knives and "collecting" them. When we went to spend the day at a flea market, he used his allowance and earned chores money to purchase three pocket knives. I was by no means keen on this idea of a 9 year old having a knife in his possession. To my protests, his oldest brother said "it's OK, he's got a collection of them at home, about seven of them!" I asked Pauly why he was collecting knives. He responded "I keep them under my pillow at night when I sleep." When I tried to gently prod for further information he shut down and responded to all my questions that he "didn't know". But I knew. Pauly was protecting himself from his molester, this monster that could appear in his life at any time and do whatever he wanted to Pauly. He didn't have the courage the first time it happened to unleash his "Power Ranger" moves on his predator. Pauly could only hope that if it happened again, this time in his own room, that he would be able to summon the courage to use his collection of knives in his defense. My heart broke in a thousand pieces.

Marvin fled in the middle of the night. He took 14 year old Joseph with him. Marvin left the area before the authorities could act. Before they could take Joseph and while he still could. They have not surfaced. But Marvin is out there somewhere. And Marvin will come back.

While Marvin drove off, he called me in an attempt to silence me again. He said, "It's in your best interest to make this go away." Before I could respond, he handed the phone to Joseph. Joseph was berserk. He raged at me, "why are you trying to ruin my life?" I knew this was my opportunity, maybe my last, to rescue Joseph as he was being driven away. I said, "Joseph, where are you, I'll come and get you right now." Joseph continued, "why are you doing this?" I quickly gave him my phone number and told him to call me. Then the phone went dead. My fault! My fault! My fault, I cried, just as Marvin had intended.

Chapter Eighteen
JUSTICE FOR NONE

This story has no conclusion. There is no final justice. For many of the people involved, there will never be closure. However, the reader can learn from this. The behaviors described within these pages are typical behaviors of a sociopath. Learn the patterns. Understand the manipulative behavior. Use your knowledge as a force for good.

To avoid prosecution, this predator fled, under the cloak of darkness. He ran away in the cover of the night, and is currently a fugitive from justice. Justice has not been served.

His victims in this place are free from his physical presence. They struggle to be free from his emotional entanglement. Just before his leaving, he tried again to silence his victims and their parents. "Keep your mouths shut," he advised. "Keep your own counsel. It will be in everyone's best interest to do so". Again Marvin mobilized that private list of people who had only witnessed his other side, his safe side, and asked that they defend him from the accusations of the others. Thus, they too were victimized. He systematically tried to turn family members against each other with a program of relentless lies. He tried to hide his hideous nature with a divide and conquer defense. Families today still suffer under the strain of his attack. Relationships have crumbled past repair. Reputations remain unrecognizable, honor extinguished. Many of his victims still go without help for all they have endured. Many of his victims have never been validated. Marvin left an unimaginable trail of destruction behind. He mangled lives for his amusement and pleasure. When he had sucked the last marrow from the bone of deviant pleasure, he ran into the night. He had no further use for us, after all. The bone was bare, and there were plenty of meaty bones in other places.

I am sure our bringing Marvin's deviant behavior into the light has not gone unnoticed. I am sure he has targeted us for future retribution. He has placed a bulls-eye on my forehead. He has marked others as well. I don't know what he will do to further silence us. "It's in your best interest not to talk or tell," he said. Marvin meant that. But I would add a note for Marvin. "It is in your interest never to come back here. I will talk. I will tell. I know you for the monster that you are, and I will do all I can to destroy you."

Marvin will now continue his evil activities elsewhere, unnoticed and uninterrupted, complete with a new view and new unsuspecting victims. There is no possibility of redemption. He would need a conscience to achieve redemption. Marvin will continue his behaviors, and in an increasingly disturbing manner, more frequent and callused. And now, with the stakes being even higher, the added elements of desperation regarding the necessity to silence any future victims, and his internalized rage regarding his being caught and hunted by authorities; one can barely speculate what Marvin's future plans might hold. In addition, what he might choose to do to silence his future victims. The unthinkable is entirely possible. Marvin may decide on a more reliable and permanent silencing technique. Our only hope is that interruption of his deviant acts will come soon. Maybe, ironically, interruption will occur through recognition.

I could not finish writing this without a message to the following people.

To Marvin

Let me remind you who you are. You are a monster! We know that now. "We once were blind, but now we see." Your disguise has been removed to expose your dark and fallen soul. You will forever be held accountable for your evil deeds.

To his family

To his mother and father, his brother and sister, his nieces and nephews and to his son, to all those who tried to love him no matter what, I hope for an end to your trauma, your pain, the shame, the blame, and the division of your family. I hope you will no longer be traumatized and victimized. I wish you the strength and comfort to go on.

To Joseph

Who carries the full extent of all these events as heavy burdens on his heart and soul. Because I did not know; because I did not protect you or rescue you from him, I am forever sorry. I write and dedicate this book of pain with that, and with you in mind. From this day forward, may you always have an angel by your side. May you have the strength and courage to continue on, in spite of the damage done. May your broken spirit mend, and may you dance again.

CPSIA information can be obtained at www.ICGtesting.com
Printed in the USA
BVOW08s1851060814

361947BV00011B/227/P

9 781937 520564